POEMS
NEW & NEGLECTED

LYNN HARD

ETT IMPRINT, SYDNEY

This edition published by ETT Imprint, Exile Bay 2016

ETT IMPRINT
PO Box R1906
Royal Exchange NSW 1225
Australia

This book is copyright. Apart from any fair dealing for the purposes of private study, research , criticism or review, as permitted under the Copyright Act, no part may be reproduced by any process without written permission. Inquiries should be addressed to the publishers.

Copyright © Lynn Hard, 2016

ISBN: 9781925416114 (pbk)
ISBN: 9781925416350 (ebook)

Cover courtesy the artist Garry Shead

Design by Hanna Gotlieb

POEMS
NEW & NEGLECTED

This is for the other guys in the quintet:
Duncan, Nige, Rae, and Tom...
with Cloudy Bay sittin' in. Better than poems.

Lynn
Sydney, 2016

CONTENTS

from DANCING ON THE DRAINBOARD 1992 7

Nights in the Pool 8
Life Style 8
I Know a Woman 8
To a Lady Who Does Not Like My Poetry 9
Dancing on the Drainboard 10
I Cannot Say 11
The Worlds Stopped Today 13
For My Former Wife Geraldine 14
For Bob Brissenden 15
For Helen 18
Ici Aussie 19
Chet Baker and Me 20
Dorothy Green 22
On First Seeing Sixteen Words for Water 24
My Last Vietnam Poem 3/10/1992 25
Having Stood on the Ledge 27

Epitaph	28
Li	29
Madame Rat	29
Cartoon	29
Aberration	31
Auto da Fé	32
Conceit	33
Sugar Ray	33
Late Night Tribute	34
Blues for the 4th of July	36
Lucia Seeks Her Father	38
Next to the Graveyard	40
In the Park, Old Men	42
Remembrance Day	43

from AUSTRALIA SUITE 1998 46

The Love Song of William Bligh	47
When Jesus Christ Came to Hawthorn	49
Elizabeth Two	50
Phillip, Prince Consort	53
Canning Street	54
Lament for Frank Hardy	56
Elder	59
Time Difference	63
On Asking a Question at an A.D. Hope Reading	65
The Dingo Kid	66
Brett Whiteley	68
All Thoroughbreds Are Related	70
Words	71
Sydney Harbour Bridge	73

from THE UNUSED PORTION 2013 75

My Mother 76
Occasions 78
At the Tomb of the Unknown Civilian 80
Ian Moffitt 82
Stolen Moments 83
Whisper Not 84
A Song for My Father 85
Nica's Dream 86
Milestones 88
Barbados 89
La Madelaine at Vezelay 90
The Moon 93
Thermal Barrier 93
Jack Savage 93
Vincent 96
Utrillo's People 98
Washing Up After the Last Supper 98
14 February 101
Il Postino 102
Level Crossing 104
Typewriter 107
Salome 108
Christmas at 70 110
Lucifer 111
Lucifer, God's Response 114
The Unused Portion 115
Ayrton Senna 117

NEW AND NEWISH POEMS 2015 119

The Unused Portion (Alternate Take) 120
After Neruda 121
The Peacocks 125

Killer Joe	127
Romance	128
A Letter from a Santa's Helper.	129
A Malevolence of Mynahs ...	130
A Clutter of Spiders	132
For John and Willie	134
Memories of My Mother in the Kitchen	136
At Night	137
State of the Union	138
On My 60th Birthday	140
For Eduardo Castellanos	141
Conceit Number 2	142
Pelleas and Melisande	143
Travelling Together	143
Concrete Structures	143
Noise	144
Berths	145
Man Dead, Two and a Half Years, Found in His Flat	147
Jane Grey	148
Blues for an Empty Room	150
Lies about My Parents	151
New Order	152
Requiem	154
I Thought I Heard Buddy Bolden Say	154
Jazz	155
Statuary	156
Ros	159
Things for Which There Can Be No Blame	160

FROM
DANCING ON THE DRAINBOARD
1992

Nights in the Pool

Black thoughts have I had of you
nestling close to me with your sharp edges
and well I might
being a vinyl animal
that people in bathing costumes
ride through the chlorinated night.

Lifestyle

Let us live at ease
in the pigeonholes
of the doll's house
safe
behind the unhinged doors
and sashless windows.
Continually rearranging
the mansion knick-knack
never
rising to an occasion,
never
turning down a bed.

I Know a Woman Who Is Going to Italy

I know a woman who is going to Italy
leaving this place for there
and taking with her
her Titian hair.

I have said that I love her
this is probably not so
she is just an idea of mine
that keeps occurring tomorrow and a moment ago.

Soon she will be just
another cameo face
seen only once
cut by light into the dark market place.

Ah, well, Italy is a backward spot
without culture or romance.
It is meet that my dark age
be Italy's renaissance.

To a Lady Who Does Not Like My Poetry

She does not think straight
this critic of mine,
her thought has too much grape,
not enough vine.

You cannot approach her
in the accustomed ways,
she has vacated the manor
to live in the maze.

But do not think, because of this,
that I would prefer her direct, rather than tacit.
She wears her appeal
in the same way a hussar slings his jacket.

Dancing on the Drainboard

I'm not usually up this early
when morning is footlights along the horizon
and birds
are tuning up behind the sets.

But this day
having given up trying to sleep
I left the bed
and walked out
to the kitchen

with its flat-faced appliances,
wiped-down surfaces
and stainless steel light
like a 'closed' sign
on a restaurant.

Centre stage
on the aluminium drainboard
are two blowflies
leaning together
slow dancing
to the end of their lives.

Oblivious to the fact
that the fly band
has gone home,
the fly couple,
(he in his cutaway,
she in her Persian lamb)
stagger through a staid
flytrot:

Ginger Bodgie
and Fred Despair.

Perhaps,
in tones inaudible to me
he is singing softly to her:
'Dancing on the drainboard
'til the tune ends
we're dancing on the drainboard
and it soon ends
we're waltzing in the wonder of why we're here
time hurries by
we're here and gone'.

She thinks it is the most romantic moment
of her life.

I back out quietly
to enter the rainforest of the shower,
the self-portrait of the mirror;
leaving them
to die with gravity.

I Cannot Say

I cannot say
what other men desire
in women,

what causes
the meetings
beyond the first,

but I
am attracted
to the lady fading.

With her beauty
like a dropped vase
and the seam
between glaze and clay
evident,

it is then,
if there is to be any style
beyond fashion,
any utility to the style,
that it may be found,

it is then,
when she is deciding
on what to jettison
like an overburdened vessel
that she may most rewardingly
be boarded.

It is then,
midst all the confusion,
her vulnerability an innocence,
that one may want her
for her previous, aging youth
or her present youthful age.

The Worlds Stopped Today

The worlds stopped today
the whole juggling act
tranced and all the balls held.

Rows of water
are caught poised
in a lake
like a mad Venetian's
blue-glass doodlings.

A poor pigeon,
being merely a cog of spring,
is fastened in endless courtship:
the hen forever turned away
from his magenta gestures.

Trees bend
at their subtle hinges:
effortlessly
mannequin.

The wind has to hold everything,
let nothing loose,
be like a man
sitting on pearls.

The sun is still
against the fabric sky
scorching it pale
and pressing our shadows
onto the grass
as indelible as clover.

The worlds stopped today
and this entire earth is as frozen, dumb
as its polar tips.

The worlds stopped today
and shall only move again
at the nudge of your lips.

For My Former Wife, Geraldine

When you said you were dying
I wondered 'all the wounds or just one?'
and I thought of old fire fights
we'd been in:
some as allies,
some as foes,
but
we're all mercenaries
and a change of side
is inevitable.

However,
since that final coat
turning
we've campaigned in separate theatres
with different decorations,
remote places of battle
and I,
for one,
have left the dispatches unread.

Until, my dear,
that last laconic message

all
in the clear
recalled
some treaties yet unbroken,
some hill we still hold
and I see us
in our uniforms of ten years ago,

I turn
at the end of business
to find you waiting
to begin the evening with me
your hair a crumpled russet curtain,
your eyes seeing more of me than there is to be seen
you say "Hello Lynn"
and I say "Hello Geraldine".

For Bob Brissenden

He was the last
of his kind
in this city
of printed instructions,
pre-stressed concrete,
artificial lakes,
and friends of the Gallery
(a place more veneer than Mahogonny).
He didn't bother
to hide his life under a bushel
and finally
his life didn't stop,
it simply ran off the road
on the way to the next experience.

I knew him only at the end,
when Parkinson's
disease and/or law
had smudged him
made the body too small
so that it shook
like the frame of a family compact
over a racing engine.
But, he was always
a taller,
straighter presence:
a truth
that the telling could not belittle.

We used to rendezvous for lunch
at Chez Moustache
like wartime agents
using the afternoons
to free ourselves
of the parachutes,
uniforms,
inflatable rafts:
forging new papers,
wondering when the underground
would make contact.

And now I know
that that last lunch
was the last,
that the rest of that afternoon
will not rest,
that the incomplete farewell
was, after all,
quite complete.

At this hour today
there happen to be weightless astronauts
tinkering in their orbital tool shed,
now and then
noticing
clouds making the world
a tiffany lamp:
they will be giddy when they land.

While in Canberra
the hours after lunch
recede
down the vacant,
perspective lines of streets
like a theory of big bang
and flocks of cockatoos
move, with the sound of nails
being pried from boards,
from tree to tree
buskering them
with white buttons.

And throughout Chez Moustache
the serviettes
stand serried, starched and white:
upright for the fallen;
another shade,
Johnny Hodges,
plays for one less:
and
all the splendid words
of the remittance man
are on their own.

For Helen

As if switching on a piece
of outmoded technology
I commence my day of work

and directed thoughts begin moving painfully through my
brain,
like a lumpy tape
drawn through a swollen and aching
recorder.

Like Sacco-
or was it Vanzetti?-
I think about spending my life
standing at street corners
talking to scorning men

'til I condense the day
into a square black briefcase
and take it home
finally turning
onto the glidepath of our driveway,
coming to a stop
before the raised drawbridge
of the garage
without a wonder to my name.

Then you
bustle these thoughts aside
and on a blank wall somewhere
a black and white newsreel
flicks on
of a tall, thin man in a suit

whirling in the street,
holding his hat,
dancing down the tramlines:
celebrating the beginning of a peace.

Ici Aussie
for Jean Paul and Monique Delamotte

In June in Boulogne by the Bois
the nights are short
and astronomers, nightingales and vampires
must take either their rest
or chances.

Lots of daylight
to watch
from the window
the workings of the courtyard:
the tenants
mostly foreign, still in the migratory process,
following the paths
past the roses
and half trees
like shabby jewels
in a Swiss movement.

Outgoing
with their string bags of intent;
and last words;
incoming
with biplane struts of baguette,
a bulge of what's on special today,
something in their eyes

about what was out of stock
and their next words.

The Conversations
are caught
in the seamless, right-angled
yard
drifting in the air
shifting like old newspapers
in the corners.

The gardienne and her assistant
have grown old in their jobs
tending the paths
heaping stuff at the feet of trees
moving the trash out each day
with the sound of tumbrils.

It's 10
and the night comes again:
time for a last look at the courtyard
and the plants in their places.
That they don't move
is their solution
to the maze.

Chet Baker and Me

The fingers pressed the valves of the horn
like the long ringing of a door bell
and
the sound from the trumpet

rushed past me like another weather.

Even now, 50 years after,
it's always a cloudless blue day at the beach
when I hear Chet Baker play;

the sun rippling like water
on the hoods and trunks of the '55 Chevy's,
the chrome fences of bumper
too bright to bear.

We all wanted to be Chet Baker
the looks, the voice,
the detachment that was attached,
living a life without vibrato.

We copied him
as if this unlettered lesson could be learned.

Eventually we all learned other lessons
and Chet was left with his finger on the bell.

In Amsterdam,
a life of back against the wall
ended
when the wall was a window.

The last flight was a fall
to lie on the film strip of the sidewalk
for careful citizens of the Netherlands
to pick their way past.

The beach at Hermosa,
the sand dinted with footprints,
is empty;
the sky a hardtop blue, scratched with contrails;
the waves skid in
showing white like light under a door

and I finish this
in my office in Australia
deep in the opposite season.

Dorothy Green

I went to buy her library.
Every space of wall
in her government house
was books,
the coloured spines
like medal ribbons.

She was small:
an aged kitten
willing to play
if asked,
but, sometimes fierce
with pain.

She resembled
her appearance
less
than anyone I've known,

it was as if the set
had been designed
without knowledge of the play.

I asked
if she'd read all the books
"No
I'd planned to do that
in my retirement"
said this lady with merry eyes
and clenched teeth.

She weakened
with each visit
until, arrangements reached,
books removed
I saw her no more.

And now,
though sad at the loss,
I am more curious
about the need
for this small person
to bear the enormous apparatus
of pain
and responsibility
and medically induced humiliation
with such civility:
struggling to pour the tea each time I called,
guilty
at not having finished
everything.

On First Seeing Sixteen Words for Water
for Billy
(Sixteen Words for Water is a play by Billy Marshall-Stoneking about the confinement
by the US government of Ezra Pound in a mental institution from 1945 to 1958)

For the old man on the stage
the season
is fall and all around him,
as if thoughts were deciduous,
lie the crumpled drafts.

Beard toward the typewriter:
a tabernacle
of old arched keys,
he waits
for the play to start.

The women,
trim and chimerical,
begin to arrive
to hear the tales of the siege,
the miracles on the walls,
the sorties almost to the sea,
the last of the rats
eaten.

Beleaguered in his asylum
for 13 years
forced to economies,
squeezed by surveillance
to a hatred of waste
the old man strips off in the desert
and closely inspects
the graffiti of the illiterate.

What is madness anyhow?

The crowd
ringing the fortress
stand among their rusted ironies of engines
and watch
the old man
thickening the walls,
stone
by
stone,
leaving no room
for a garrison.

My Last Vietnam Poem 3/10/92
(On the occasion of the dedication of the Australian Vietnam War Memorial)

In that vestibule
of war
among the potted
napalms

we would send in our body bags
and medals
would come back

rows of transistors
on our uniforms
giving us the look
of down-at-heal androids

and now
we've got a monument.

I liked it better without the monument.
Before
at least 'Nam was real.
An unfinished,
desperate kind of thing
that was probably
still going on

but now,
we've got a monument
like the other wars do.
A compact, neatly designed,
glossy,
happy ending,
for the blokes to visit
with their families,
their partly-paid for camper vans,
their BMWs,
their paunches,
their wheelchairs,
and all the other things
we didn't have

when
like a big
cowboy rope trick
the rotors whirled
faster and faster
'til the insects
would wobble off
and tail up
scoot
to their acronym
with me
sitting in the door,

gripping the gun,
watching the world
fast-forward by

in a compartment
crewed by men,
not one of whom still exists:
young, lean, utilitarian men
with no investments and no debts,
who wouldn't visit monuments
even if they could.

Having Stood on the Ledge

Having stood on the ledge
and watched the crowd gather
in anticipation
of splatter,
I know the indifference to height,
that the ledge
is an improvement
on the hotel room
and its special channel
that endlessly rolls the time,
the weather
and the wind direction by,
and I know the indifference to the street:
just another cord in the net.

Having taken the step
and felt my intestines
uncoiled by gravity
I have dropped

like a fluttering x,
a dark cross of St. Andrew,
watching the crowd
make a place for me.
The awnings flash by:
Blurs of test patterns,
Lodgers gouached by the tube
do not look up
from loving Lucy,
they go past like credits
scrolling up.
I drop,
my clothes make an annoying buffet,
and worse,

the street gets no nearer.

Epitaph

Michelangelo Buonarroti
has granted a final boon,
accepted his last commission:
gone to finish the moon.

Li

In one life
a man could not see
all the citizens of China
if they lined up
and marched past.

I have placed my chair
near the willow,
I trust
you will not be the last.

Madam Rat

Madam Rat:
How clever of you to note,
during my direst peril,
that it was exactly the removal of your weight
that would keep me afloat.

Cartoon
for Alex Skovron

Disney
would have loved it
the Chink
dancing
with the jolly tank.

Textured
backgrounds of carved posts,
curved roofs,
red tiles

cute,
easily drawn
exotic.

Uncle Walt
supervising everything:
the score
(lots of gongs),
the plot line
(straight as a dropped anvil)
snatching
the transparent out-takes
(Tianamen
Chow Mein
and rows of bicycles
like broken spectacles)
and dropping them
from the animator's desk
to the cutting room floor.

One image persists:
the fortunate student
disappearing
like a Chinese coyote
under the tank,
staring up,
amazed,
as disillusionment, maturity and life pass over him
in quick succession.

It's good TV:
Mickey introduces
Tinkerbell who introduces
Goofy who introduces
'Adventures in Liberty'
to us,
the unfortunate,
who have to wait
for theirs.

Aberration

Am I wrong?
All this Time?
Maybe life
isn't a lumpen
interruption to an eternal zing!
A crow
sagging the longest distance
telephone wire.

Maybe,
maybe
it's an opportunity
to climb into a high tech Formula One
and win
at Le Mans

and stand on a high place
shaking
that cricket bat-shaped bottle,
spraying
ferment
on those who didn't enter.

Auto-da-Fé

To call the Arians,
the Cappadocians,
the Copts,
the Albigensians,
heretics
is not to know the true nature
of transgression.

They had solutions
and expected from them
predictable outcomes.
Hope,
in other words.
The true heretic
has fallen out with hope,
he must have
certitude
either in nothing
or in all.

Hope,
being merely boarded-up logic,
is too make-
shift.

And so I seek certitude
in love
like an augurer
looks for signs.
Novices, initiates, priestesses
propagate your faith
(and incidentally notice

I wear my sanbenito with a certain
rake).
It were a shame
to let me go by
and tie myself up
at another's stake.

Conceit

Should my love become a star
she would shed such light
that wisemen would lose their wits
and Christ be born every night.

Sugar Ray

Sugar Ray Robinson
is
pound for pound
the deadest fighter in the world.

The tape
has stopped rolling
and the editing
process has begun.

Lazarine:
The puzzled bloated figure rising,
walking rapidly
backwards,
rewinding
past spectator,

ringside,
towel-necked handler,
getting off the floor
blacker,
neater,
answering every bell.

Cut it there.
Freeze
on the champ
gloves clasped over his head
like a Sugar Ray Robinson wristwatch
telling us it's noon
or midnight.

You'll have to go outside
to tell.

Late Night Tribute

One of those figures
clustered about the Duesenberg,
its hood like a nightclub awning,
in an ad
in 'Vanity Fair'.

A line drawing
in Webster's
defining the definition
of debonair.

A spatted,
morning-suited messenger

passing out lined leaflets
by Yiddish migrants
to avenues of shabby men:
spring in his step
and his boutonniere.

A saviour of sorts,
dancing for our sins,
as if America
were light on its feet,
tireless and spare.

On his arm
the ultimate male chauvinist remark:
no matter
if it's Ginger, Cyd
hat rack,
or chair.

Moving through life
with the wind behind him,
pulling out
and passing despair,
an angle
signed against the air:

Fred Astaire.

Blues for the 4th of July

When the Canberra Times gives the score
baseball teams
sometimes beat basketball teams;
the Rose Bowl
is never mentioned;
there are letters to the Editor questioning
the use of 'world'
in World Series.
People say 'Yank'
as if you've just gotten out of an Edsel;
conversations with telephone operators
are Abbott and Costellian;
and taxi drivers have asked me for 13 years
how I like Australia.

They tell me Nabokov
spoke with an accent
all his life;
Roy Eldridge
went to bed the world's best trumpet player
and woke up old fashioned
with gigs hard to get till he died.
And he never could
play bop.

Sometimes in July,
when it feels like Christmas,
and I've just picked my morning foreign paper
off the lawn
and the news
is all
about some place else

I know
I'm not in the driver's seat
or inside the carriage either,
more a postillion,
not
even a horse.
I walked out in the middle
of the Hollywood movie
and came in too late
at the pickies
to know who did it
or
why

so I charge as much as I can
to American Express,
send poems to American expatriates
(each from a different country),
and ignore
two mismatched trees:
one a tall, silver maple
that the wind pulls shut
like a blind,
the other a squat, dreadlocked
willow
and
a space of grass
I used to mow weekly:
I have been across Australia
to Ayres Rock
the Kimberleys,
and crossed the Nullarbor Plain
and seen nothing
so vast.

Lucia Seeks Her Father

I was in Riga last week
for the first time since 1938
and
I looked for you.

Except
for your absence
not much has changed in Riga.

The train station,
an ornate shed over the weather,
made to house shadows and drafts and hide
the dirt,
is as I remembered it:
a great barn of loss

and our street
has most of the same houses,
in their windows
the reflections
have stayed in my thoughts

and the post office
at the square
is repainted
a new, glossy colour
so thick over the doors
and window sashes
that it seemed
sealed.

And I wondered
what they did
with all those thin blue letters I sent here,
what they did
with all those thick cream packets
you posted to me.

I left Riga,
as one does in 1989,
by an ever accelerating plane
straining at my seat belt
to watch the city
until the last edge of its street map
dropped from the corner
of my cell-like window.

Then I sat back
and looked in perfect hatred
at the golden-coiffed, uniformed
stewardesses
dispensing food.

But life
is full of coincidence
and today
in Jerusalem,
I heard your name
at the Yad Vashem
memorial.

The voice reciting the names
among the candles
said it:

your name
just after Uncle Yeshev,
your name
just before
my sister.

Next to the Graveyard

Out of town,
waiting for a taxi,
sitting on a fence
by a graveyard
full of strangers,
I take stock,
the internal telephone exchange
has gone quiet
and for the moment
I am alone.

Do good fences
make good neighbours?
This border
between absurdities
says:
'Leave them alone,
they have returned',
they are boat people
no longer.

Whitman's grass
is so thorough,
so flawlessly green
that I envy the animals

who can eat it.
The rows of weathered head stones,
like the keys
of an old cash register,
neatly assemble
the discarded suits of clothes:
a formation of old uniforms,
a buried op-shop.

Each stone is a goodbye card
with a verse,
a sentiment.
For many
the only poem in their life
and they'll never
read it.

In the growing seasons
the caretaker
comes every day
and mows
in the minds
of the grievers.

At this foreign location
it is a fine, spring day
and perched on the frame
of this place
I notice
over the road
thin, pale gums
angling across a dark copse
like Uccello's lances.

The taxi keeps me idling here
but I am content
with time to seriously consider
jumping down from my fence
and standing upright
so that the sky
can stain my hair blue.

In the Park, Old Men

Brass-chested summer
hovers on membraned wings
above the foliaged park.
Away from the sun's
predatory teeth
old men group in shade.
Within the park's twig-wickered cage
they sit huddled on slatted perches,
shawled and quiet like covered parrots,
watching the magenta-smudged pigeons
prance out
their music hall turns.

As if getting used to the dark
the old men wait
until the sun
returns to hang in his cave.
Alighting from benches
they walk concrete limbs
out to the park margin
past used pigeons strewn like moultings,
on the grass.
There the inflexible soldier is,
rifle held like some boatman's oar,

veteran against envy,
decorated with bird lime:
the black-and-white ribbon
of resolve.

Remembrance Day

Bugger it
and over the top,
chancing a life
presumed lost;
holding his breath
as the gas
smears past;
exhausted
from resisting elemental impulses;
gone mad
digging.

For this:
a place in the parade
on Remembrance Day,
a weak grip
at one end of a banner
opposite
another brittle figure
with outsized ears and oversized clothes:
the two
and the silk
a kind of coat of arms
for an infirm family.
They parade
from the assembly point
to the place of homage

before the polished fortress,
the hyperbolied grave.
At the very last
they totter the same
ground weapons the same
at ease
the same
as at the end
of a route march
in France.

The speeches
are the kind
the permanent
give to the transient
and the faces of the veterans
concentrate,
listening for something
they might have missed:
their former
front-line indifference
lost with the fit of their clothes
and all the other options.

The day
fades
and the screens pop on
in all the darkened
living rooms,
like windows in boats
over the reef.
And the ranks
of rumpled grey figures
climb jerkily again
from the sharply incised trenches,

with their burdens of boxy packs
looking more like bearers than hunters,
and scurry off
diminishing in perspective.
In the most random
way
some, now and then,
fall over.

And behind
in the chambers
of the trenches
cups cool,
candles time-lapse away
ink dries:
the Mary Celeste scene
at the back of the battle
always there
always there
always waiting there.

At the farthest edge of the advance
almost
at the point of perspective
the rite of remembrance
is finished.
They read the rock rosters
of their regiments
that lack
their names
and are forced
to follow on:
war to the knife,
fighting
to the last man.

FROM
AUSTRALIA
SUITE
1998

The Love Song of William Bligh

In 1806 William Bligh arrived in Australia to take up duties as Governor. His daughter Mary and her husband accompanied him. His wife Elizabeth's health would not permit her to come. In addition to the Bounty mutiny, Bligh was known in the navy as a brilliant navigator and cartographer having served as Captain James Cook's sailing master on his third and last voyage. He also commanded vessels in the Battles of Camperdown and Copenhagen earning praise from Nelson. Throughout his career Sir Joseph Banks was his untiring patron. Bligh was ousted from the Governorship by the "Rum Rebellion" and held in house arrest until 1808. He left Australia in 1810. During the remainder of his naval career he was promoted twice to finally reach the rank of Vice Admiral.

Adrift on the Southern sea
with a mutinous crew:
this is nothing new, my dear.

Not very different from the Bounty
its deck an orchard of breadfruit,
at day's end the spirit level sun
blackening our side of the islands
like characters in a native shadow play

or Cook
dying on the sand,
his rescue
backing water beyond the Father Christmas surf,
blaming me at Deptford Hard.

Of course, our Mary's here
loyal, as your daughter would be,
where, before I have been alone.
But, as before
and always,

I am outnumbered
and she is beset by the odds
distracting me when I must not waver

for those of us who are truly of the service know
that often success doesn't encompass succeeding,
but it ever entails the discernment of duty.

I am called harsh, intemperate, uncompromising
when it is known that I flog little,
bear no grudges,
speak fairly with men who are inferior in ability to me,
and can, in all cases,
be counted upon to finish my tasks.

Ah well, Elizabeth, I keep on,
trusting the Admiralty and Banks
and, of course,
you my dear
to know my accusers are enemies
and men who rather than rising up the captains' list,
wish to have it come down to them.

Oh, but sometimes Mrs Bligh
even with my skill as a navigator
I despair of setting a proper course.

Nor would I, without you
for what good
is the base line of the horizon,
the buoys of the stars,
the deeps and shallows of my charts,
without a position to sail to,
a place to find?

When Jesus Christ Came to Hawthorn

When Peter Hudson, the full-forward for Hawthorn, was Australian Rules most famous footballer, a grafitti in a Hawthorn pub asked : "What would you do if Jesus came to Hawthorn?" Someone chalked a reply : "Move Peter Hudson to half-forward."

He was welcome
though he looked more Jewish
than his pictures,
and
as long as he didn't jump the queue.

He could catch the shuttle to the casino
and chase the money changers out of the temple,
at closing time.

He could cross Power Street against the light
if he didn't attract a following.

He could recite with the performance poets at the Town Hall
and come fourth,

He could turn water into wine,
but he wouldn't please everyone.

He could ride Simpson's donkey
in the Anzac Day parade.

And if he really wanted to eat his last supper
he could have a counter meal at a pub in Burwood Road.

He could get arrested,
and meet the local Sanhedrin and the Magistrate in Charge of Injustice.

He could drag his cross down Church Street
from tram stop to tram stop.

He could die of indecision
at the intersection of Bridge Road, Burwood Road and Church Street
with a few pedestrians looking on
confused by the colosseum noises from Glenferrie Oval
announcing the apotheosis of Peter Hudson.

Or,
He could live
in the wilderness.

Elizabeth Two

Queens don't carry money
which is a shame
because it's personalised, you know,
my picture on every coin and note,
not that you could recognise me
from the likeness
it's me as I was in the fifties:
just crowned,
touring the colonies
visiting Australia.
A procession of beginnings,
they even held things up
so I could start them.
Time seemed a mirage then:
only mid-day shadows,
everyone in their best clothes,
the little girls with flowers,
the newly painted Aborigines

their rude bits covered
with new tops and shorts,
the sprinklers left on overnight
to green up the lawns in the outback towns
like grass stains on riding britches,
the provincial military
clayed and polished
to their maximum potential,
in short,
more majeste
than less.

It's changed now.
After all,
it is difficult to play the same
part
for forty years
no one else is asked to go on
unaltered
year after year.
One looks
different,
I worry about being an aging rock star
rather than
Vera Lynn
I worry that my unroyal and royal
lives
continue to diverge
and it's harder to call them both real.

My family
wants it all,
privilege and
freedom

and all they've got
is a reciprocal relationship
with the gutter press
and Australia
has so fallen away
that the country entire
wants to immigrate from me.
I wonder do they see
that I don't have that privilege?
A part of my Queendom,
my burden,
is Australia:
always was,
always will be.
The relationship is fixed:
they the subject,
I the predicate
in an ancient sentence.

You see,
a monarchy, as old as this one,
cannot advance
but must simply withstand
siege after siege.
Its fortress
is like a folly
in the gardens;
remove one stone
and the ruin is real.

Philip, Prince Consort

My life
is like a sound wave
at the point
where sound no longer carries.
It has run out of resonance
and I who reside in this life
can only cross my legs and
stir the lees of being a gentleman.
All I've accomplished
is to keep my part
of the bargain.

God, it almost makes me understand
feminists

but it's a job
and I'm lucky to get it,
considering my background:
I can ape my ancestors
and their unearned medals,
rank,
uniforms,
titles, albeit
with more limited
whims
and I am next to her:

the queen
of a country of queens,
and that makes her
the most desirable woman in the world,
more calm than distance,

more erotic than accident,
more kind than obliging,
more complex than a trouping of the colours.

She is all these things
and I
am her consort
yet

most privately,
in that valise from my past
that I never unpack,
is a desperate wish
that in some helix of time
we would meet,
say at court

she with nothing but her charm
and a tray of oranges held just
below her neckline
and I with favours to bestow:
encourtiered,
peruked,
cavalier,
saturnine.

Canning Street
For Frank Hardy

An old street map
would do
for walking through
North Carlton.

There's a quiet
about the trees
and neatly piled bricks of buildings
that isn't today
or yesterday
but more
the day before.

Where the street turns
like an old fashioned
dance step
the papers in the newsagency
have simply
had their dates put forward.

The footpaths
are too uneven
to be current,
the architecture has no independent lines
the houses designed
to tolerance
of their neighbours.

On an elevated, flat place
a sign,
barely flaking,
has been painted on the bricks
urging us
to buy
a product
that no one can pay for
anymore.

Overall,
there is a sense
that people live alone here:
going away each morning
returning in the evening
to put the kettle on
and tell the truth
to themselves.

Lament for Frank Hardy

The funeral began
with us all singing "Waltzing Matilda"
though many, including myself, knew only
the more obvious words.

Frank,
who talked such a high percentage
and just managed to meet his small quota for listening,
was quiet in his box.

My 76 year old Felix Randal
had died, form guide in hand:
the bottom end of a quinella.
His life,
made up of idea
rapidly followed by action
(except in those many cases where action didn't wait)
was for some reason,
over.

An earlier stroke
had put a great sadness on him

sorry
to finally accept
that the game went on
but not the players.

To me,
a younger man,
Frank
was not like anyone else.
Age had not blurred him
like some statue weathered in a garden,
the vandals
broke their hammers on his nose.

With a voice like the scratch of a match
he spoke with an accent of another time
a time that was shared out among the people
with their sharp newsreel faces,
parted hair and hoarded clothes.
Not like our time
which is reserved for a few
who are rounded like dolls
with suits always on the verge
of going out of fashion.

And he is gone now,
all his furniture empty,
his autobiography ended on an early
act of defiance,
his cat fostered out,
his pipe cold.

At the funeral
the attendance was large

and the speakers spoke well of him in his many parts
but frankly
there didn't seem to me to be any Frank there:
no overwhelming smell of tobacco,
no red socks,

until,
as the casket was being taken away,
the local Trades Hall Choir
filed in to sing the "Internationale".
There were a dozen or so
dressed come as you are,
all ages, all sizes,
one woman nursing a baby,

and it was as if,
for an instant,
the figures in the "Night Watch"
had stilled their separate actions
to tell Rembrandt
goodbye,

as I must,
I suppose.
But, of course, you know, Frank,
any time you ask
I'll come a waltzin' matilda
with you.

Elder

When something different happened
there was always one of us
who in their memory had known it to happen before
because,
as long as time,
the water, the air, the land had been part of the people's knowledge
and even when,
in the sky,
the spirits beyond us
made a rare, miraculous exposure
of themselves
that was not in the people's knowledge
it never lasted,
never changed anything,
the miraculous always passed

and we spun
in the net that the night showed us
without end:
a distant spider
mid many distant spiders
until

the ones who made things
came.

When I first saw them
I thought "they will kill all of us"
in the same way
they had killed the sea
and the horizon.
In the same way the things they made

killed the land.
In the same way
they made any of our truths that left them out
lies.
How could the people stop them
if the spirits could not?
What I had first seen
as unnatural and blasphemous
I came to see as proof
that they were stronger
than what the people knew.
That their strength
was strong everywhere
and ours ...?
Oh, we knew that they were animals as we were,
that beyond their paths they became lost
that they were not always brave
or aloof
or immune to injury or death,
that they coupled with our women
and that they were few
but
they had such knowledge
that ours
was not even the earliest part of it,
ours
was not part of it all.
They did not barter with the land
they ordered it and it obeyed
just as they used the sea and the air.
Their knowledge was so large
it could not be shared.
They had people who only fought and thought about fighting,
who only traded and thought about trading,

who only punished and thought about punishment,
who were only punished and thought about not being punished.

How could the people,
whose knowledge was too small
to separate,
defeat the ones who made things?
It was as if we had finally encountered
one of those distant bright spiders
from another part of the net.

When I first saw them
I thought "they will kill all of us"
but they didn't.
Just the ones on the easy part of the land
but they didn't kill all of us,
but they didn't let us live either.

They didn't kill us
but they didn't take us in
they left us in the hard places
they didn't want
to live with corrupted beliefs
and partial solutions.

I was so ashamed.
Humiliated that, in all the time before,
we had never questioned,
never done more than modify what we found,
never seen our ability to think
as a mandate to make,
to differ,
to be one of the people yet more,
and so I couldn't resist,
yet, couldn't accept.

Now,
the shame is past.
We do see these things,
we see the edges of the knowledge of the others,
we understand the makings of things
and seek our place.
But what we have learned
has divided us:
we know it is only distance
that makes the night seem unchanged
and we know (yes, we know)
that the times of the unmarked sea
cannot be lived in again.

But it is those times
and the smudged knowledge of those times
that we must rely on,
even with its accompanying burden
of a communal suspension of disbelief,
for there is no accommodation
with those who make,
no useful understanding to be reached
with this ungenerous, dying tribe
whose obsession with making
has eliminated use.
They have lost what they had to give us
and broken what we had.

When I first saw them
I thought "they will kill all of us".

Time Difference

At tea time
we all settle down before the evening news,
like the tribe around the camp fire,
to watch little figures
act out the world
for us.

It's always the ABC for us:
I don't believe it seemly
to interrupt the major players
with people leaping beside their cars
or deciding on home loans.

Tonight,
one of the players is our Foreign Minister
who spoke at the United Nations today.
He came on after pictures
of dental decay in the buildings of what was Yugoslavia
and was followed
by Giacometti children in Africa.

In between
the minister
disguised within his suit and beard,
speaks over scenes of piles of skulls in the jungle,
like statuary in a garden gone mad,
to the might of the world
about his alternative plan for making
Cambodia a level playing field.
Cut to
the diplomats
listening attentively
behind their name plates.

Of course,
there's the time difference.
None of this is really happening.
In New York it's deep night
the process of civilisation
has been stopped (maybe for us to catch up).
At the U.N.
the lights are switched off,
the seats closed
like obstinate mouths
and outside
the wind,
another level of river,
moves by.
Vacant flag poles,
their halliards thumping
like the British archers
nervously plucking their bow strings
before Agincourt,
line the street before the closed book
of the building.
Only the inscriptions,
defaced by the dark,
hint at the purpose
of the structure.

The moon
is a spotlight
in an old prison movie
moving across the city
looking into every hiding place,
entering the bedrooms

of the minister
and the delegates,
turning the sleeping heads
to ash.

But at home,
we've passed by the sports and weather,
and the news and the ABC is done.
Leaving us
to the reruns
of sitcoms, soaps, and movies
from other continents
within the ever escalating fantasy
of the television night

that someone
has already lived in.

On Asking a Question at an A.D. Hope Reading*
*At this time, Prof. Hope was extremely hard of hearing

"Ahem, Professor Hope, if you please,
would you tell me why Abelard, why Eloise?"
and though I spoke directly in his ear
Professor Hope affected not to hear.

Again, more loudly, I stated my query
drowning, not waving in a sea of theory
Professor Hope, ineffably kind,
looked at me as if I were losing my mind.

Once more, shouting, I questioned the text:
why bring in this example of antique, but safe sex?

But as with the oysters, answer came there none
and frankly, I thought my course had been run

when another of the listeners in the politest way
restated, with a different accent, what I had to say
and it was clear the Professor had at last got my gist
but from the look on his face I knew there was something I'd missed.

"Ah Sir, you have misunderstood that part
it's not about those two but an old affair of my heart"
when pressed to name her he would not:
perhaps I was too prurient, or maybe he just forgot

but whatever the case it is not my purpose to malign
for if most lives are vinegar, his was wine
and now when it grows quiet below the belt and above the knees
I, too, often think of Abelard and Eloise.

The Dingo Kid

I'm the real symbol of Australia

not the poofter kangaroo
bouncing around
with its family in the glove box
bloody hell, it doesn't even eat meat!
Or the old maid emu:
a bird!
A non-flying bird!
About as useful as a peace-time army.
If they weren't protected they'd be extinct

and don't even bloody mention
the koala:

a hand puppet as a national emblem
of the angriest country in the world
(you know there's more anger on a Saturday night
in a Newcastle suburb
than you'll find in a whole American CBD
come off it!

It's me
the dingo,
the bushranger dog.
I'll kill your stock,
I'll take your children
and I'm hell on rabbits.

Crikey, they built a fence
across half the country
just to keep me out.

I'm native,
I'm mean,
I'll eat anything that's different,
I don't vote 'cause I won't
give anybody
my approval
but I'm not bigoted,
I'll give everything a go.

So here's what it comes down to:
who'd you rather have
represent you when the carnivores gather
and national pride's on
the line?

The Dingo Kid
or fuckin' Skippy?

Brett Whiteley

I only met him once
at Nick Pounder's bookshop in the Cross
he was buying a book
on Marsden Hartley
and I was drunk
from a long lunch.

He seemed to like that,
as we talked about Hartley
and another strange American,
Ryder,
who painted and repainted his pictures
'til they cracked,
seemed to like it that
I had drunk to be vulnerable.

He bought a book
and left
and I paid
a lot more attention to his work
than I had before
wishing I could do in a poem
what he did in a painting
just drop in a tit
or a bum
rounded to its apogee
and change the flavour of the work
entirely.

I found
his pictures
to have an acceleration

of their own
the curves and swoops
imparting a snap the whip
chain reaction
like the wheels and gears
in a 17th century
perpetual motion machine.
It's not surprising
he covered the walls of a room
with a painting:
the larger the machine
the more difficult to detect
its futility.

On the day his death was announced
I thought of the small man
in the bookstore
grinning up at me
with curls like the foam on a beer mug
and I imagined him
when the blue
could get no deeper
and all the degrees of the
arc were used

lying in a bed in a motel
from his American period
close to the surf
whose restlessness
shows that
even the sea has doubts

and on the table next to his bed
a syringe of the afternoon,

a bottle of the weekend,
and on his easel
a shopping list
for the rest of his holiday.

All Thoroughbreds are Related

At Randwick,
a jockey's off,
down
on the deep green grass
like pigment squeezed from a tube.

Attendants
are rushing toward him;
an ambulance
pulls out on to the track
in a wide arc

and riderless,
away,
the horse runs loose
bursting through a barrier
flying up the straight
with a vacant back,
stirrups bouncing rhythmically
like pedals
free wheeling

galloping faster
in anarchy
than ever in any handicap
he passes the mirrored finish line

grinning through his bit
and doesn't slow
flashing by the railed in punters

so imbued with their servitude
that as liberation blurs by
they tear up their betting slips without defiance,
just a vague resentment of those
who run but don't race,
and return to a place in the queues
to buy another ticket
for another small trip
to where they will never go.

Epilogue

The horse
is no good for racing again
and lives out his life
losing his figure
under his favourite tree:
fucking,
not running,
for money.

Words
For Bob Ellis and Anne Brooksbank

Words
over Palm Beach
burning in the air:
Bob Ellis's house
went up in flames the other night

making a beacon
for mariners
and others.

Cast for once
in a big budget, action feature
he ranged over the set
uncertain
of his role
constantly changing focus:
Lear,
Loman,
The Prince.
Finally sure
at the point of realisation
he plays a supporting part.

Probing
the strangers crowded around,
the lights on the fire engines
pirouetted endlessly,
overhead the press
in a helicopter
its rotor turning like a tap in the sky,
sprayed the area
with curiosity.

Being known
there are no havens
from disaster
except the affection of your friends.

On the height
the shadow the old house had hid
for many years

is now exposed.
Thumbprint
pressed on a document,
and the sea,
Bob's closest, most senior neighbour
knows him for the first time
without the protection of its walls.

In a positive gesture
it nods
backward and forward
to say that nothing
has changed.

Sydney Harbour Bridge

The harp of the south,
the first real evidence
to the world
(or maybe just England)
that there was creation down here
as well as discovery.

Built by the workers,
opened by Fascists,
crossed by people who live out of town,
it is one of the unsurprising things
that tourists
want to take back with them
rolled up in their cameras;
crossing their bosoms on T-shirts,
the sole useless
item on their key chains,

a ceramic span bearing the traffic of hot house fish
on the bottom of a Kansas aquarium.

The bridge
is a silent object
subjugated to the lands it links,
a completed answer to the problem,
a frozen ferry ride
and,
it must be said,
as with many structures,
it was more interesting
incomplete.
Its mythical tusks,
those straining reaching arms
seemed to grow out of the minds and emotions
of a generation

until they closed
to form a hoop
for the sea to jump through.

FROM
THE UNUSED PORTION
2013

My Mother

My mother was someone I knew well
as a child.
We lived in the same houses
and met frequently,
though, seemingly, always to my disadvantage.

And in the last, tense years of my youth
I spent most of my time
manoeuvering against her:
the eating of the cake
assured,
I wanted possession now.

She was like some garden
I threshed about in,
careless of the trees I broke,
flowers I spoiled
confident I was not a weed.

She had my father
and books of old photographs
of which, I thought as a boy,
that if you held them upside down
time would tip out.

She had relatives she had to keep
in states she'd left behind;
beliefs she'd discarded
and others she didn't discuss.

But,
I'd won
and had begun a life-long investigation

of other women's lives
in which I would be
not so much a lover
as a naughty, foster parent;
not so much a friend
as a philanthropist.

She died this morning
and I sit in her house
late at night,
my 90 year old father having cried himself to sleep.
The furniture, objects, colours here
do not work for me.
She stood somewhere in this room
where I cannot stand
and saw from her vantage
a balance,
an apt positioning
and was pleased.

A chime
that she hung
is touched by the wind
in unresolved, hesitant whole notes
of such pure regret
that the pressure
of unused compassion
forces my fists
to my eyes,
accepting
that my crime
is no longer neglect
but loss.

Occasions
For Annette and Charles

In the mail
a wedding invitation
from two friends,
no strangers to marriage
or themselves,
who intend to marry
again.

On the cover of the invitation
Breughel's peasants
dance the kermess
accelerating through the patterns
peculiar to their idea of order.

The confusions of war
fret the northern horizon,
a cold front bringing a late frost approaches from the west,
and, all unsuspected,
the year's first case of plague
just disembarked in distant Genoa.

But just now
the four horsemen
have tethered their mounts outside
to await the end of the occasion.
Glad, no doubt,
to rest their features from grimacing,
their thews from riding,
to lean back against a tree
and close their eyes,
awful implements laid aside.

In the midst
of their short unhappy lives
the dancers
continue the kermess,
forming a circle like a wall,
kicking up their skirts,
following their codpieces 'round,
grabbing a tousle headed mug,
crumbling a pie over their front.

They are not lost,
they know where they are.
They don't have our mass media
to delude them that life is anything
but a descent.
They have a church
that sees it as a cost
in an elaborate cost-benefit analysis.

And on occasion
sometimes at a wedding
they dance,
flinging onto the scales,
that eternally shrug one shoulder,
their paltry coins:
stolen from the eyes of the dead,
gained from fucking travellers,
taken from someone else's hoard
dug-up from beneath a bush
and all,
every copper from every source open to them,
will not nudge the balance.

Yet they dance
sometimes at a wedding

and stamp the ground
to keep the old gods awake,
to keep themselves awake
ransoming back
what morality,
and convention
have stolen
following their neighbour
into the turn
knowing that the nearer to sin,
the nearer to God.

At the Tomb of the Unknown Civilian
A Poem About 9/11

On borrowed carpets,
the Arabian nights paid America a visit
a while ago
"striking the Sultan's turret with a shaft of light"
and so on.
But America survived…
well a lot of it anyway

The soldiers survived
both those in regiments
and those who raced into the nearest phone booth
to rip off their hated mufti
and reveal the uniform underneath
finding a home
in the army of reduced options.

Beginning alphabetically,
the warrior class went to Afghanistan,

but even before they'd used up every code name,
acronym and map coordinate,
they were onto the next marginal enemy.
They shipped their depleted munition stocks,
motor pools and bellicose air conditioning
to the desert next door.

But the civilians,
the professional civilians,
who, like most of the citizens of Tombstone,
didn't wear guns,
those positive symbols of a successful state,
didn't fare too well.

Going unarmoured into the marketplace
you sometimes lose.
But differently from the soldier,
who takes pride in being interchangeable.
A civilian is irreplaceable
because they make their own rituals,
traditions, if,
in fact, habit can be so glorified,
and they were lost along with their workstations, files, memos
and the photographs in their frames
when ignorance could not stand being contradicted any longer.

The unknown soldier
is dulce et decorus;
the unknown civilian
means there are only soldiers left.

Ian Moffitt

Trenchcoat weather
in Sydney,
incompleting the Harbour Bridge
and Ian Moffitt is dead
from something else
he couldn't swallow.

A foreign correspondent,
an old China hand,
there on the Yangtse
when the massive body finally rejected
the gun boat;
covering the U.N. in New York
and its abridgement:
gangland killings;
in countless capitols
seeing the heirs to the perpetual motion machine
confine their actions
to a series of small rooms;
and in many other places
known only because their absurdity
turned lethal
for the reporter's lot
is to be present where the beast
has gained control,
throwing what is at hand at other beasts,
their angels on the dole.

Ian went out from Oz
to experience the madness of others
at first hand
and thereby,

with his news and his novels
(where he put in what the world left out),
shape a good Australian.

He always seemed just returned from somewhere,
new labels and scrapes on his luggage,
but with time to fully consider you
until he left again.
His face, in repose,
was a demonstration of how to deal with danger
for, like Yeats' chinamen,
he was merry,
Oh, he was merry,
and he made me feel more confident
about us.

We shall never read his byline again
but whatever new assignments
he has gone to
he will be going in harm's way
if there is any harm to be found.

Stolen Moments
Composer: Oliver Nelson

You,
you who like to give warnings
take this as mine.

Yes you, the ones who took my time
only to misplace it somewhere in your fortified desks,
a tower of filing cabinet at each corner.

You, dressed in somebody else's taste
with no life below the keyboard
and no thoughts above.

You, who scarred the face of the sun
to make a clock;
who want every picayune from that doubloon of the day.

Take this as fair warning
that when you don't watch
or when you do

I will steal the odd moment or two,
I will steal it back

and then wander out the gate with my lunch pail
and a small fortune

to spend on a friend,
or an idea signed by the artist,
or on two words that have never met, yet rhyme,
or on an entirely different way to calculate time.

Whisper Not
Composer: Benny Golson

I won't spare your feelings
so don't you spare mine.
In fact, in this affair,
let there be no sparing at all.
Let it be shouts and song
and loud conversations in darkened apartment blocks,
whole afternoon arias of sex

penetrating the neighbors' walls
with the impact of our affection.
So speak right up,
whisper not
and all unmuffled
come formula one with me
each pushing a bare foot to the floor;
driving the course to the limit,
loving our lap times,
until, finally, concentration wavers
and we lose it leaving a chicane
coming to in the family sedan
waiting for the light to change,
the trees latticing overhead like the edging of a bank note

A Song for My Father
Composer: Horace Silver

You never met my father
if you think a song with a latin beat
is appropriate.

I've seen my father dance:
nothing moves below the waist,
not even the feet

When he's sober
it's like a dashboard figure
sliding with the turns;

When he's drunk
he bends and raises at the waist
like one of those oil pumps he used to work on,
but without as much rhythm

and the dance floor clears
and his partner just grins
and my father laughs and squeezes up his face
so that all you can see of his eyes
is a glimpse of good weather somewhere.

When I was a kid,
my father came home from the plant every night and parked in front
of the house
and argued for the working man
with the right wing commentator on the car radio.

In the depression,
when he lived on the borders of subsistence,
my father decided to subscribe to all 47 volumes of
the World's Great Literature
and my mother agreed!

Last year my father told me, in conversation,
that his sight, hearing and hair were going
and that, evidently, his heart had finally done what he never could:
produce a latin beat

and I was the only one afraid.

Nica's Dream

Composer: Horace Silver

The Baroness Pannonica Von Koenigswarter known as
"Nica" was a great friend to Jazz figures in the 40s and 50s.

I, too, knew a Baroness.
Estranged from a Baron, as it happened,
and the estates, serfs
and sundry feudal privileges.

Elegant,
with an accent
she made you feel like Bogart in Casablanca.
A Magyar:
behind her high domed cheekbones
you could see
little fellows just down from their horses:
curious, smelling of lacquer, sweat and violence.

She was as difficult
as a complicated piece of harness
and just as appealing;
spoke the languages of Europe;
knew what every Baroness should know.

The family portraits
and the bricks of the palaces might have been left behind
but not the veneer
or the table manners.

Yet this lady with a title
seemed to lack an author,
began each day with a vomit,
and slept with clenched fists,
resisting, through the night,
the invading armies of her dreams.

Living with her was like being the minister of state
of some Balkan country:
treaties endlessly negotiated,
instantly broken
and the final betrayal, while an ache,
was such a gentle defenestration
that today my memories are not of how she used a knife
but how she held it.

Milestones
Composer: Miles Davis

Trips:
the bags in the boot,
the clothes on the back seat, maps and CDs in front,
each door slams shut
and everything here is mortal, a rerun, a dropped leaf.

The movie outside the car starts running through the film gates of
the windows
faster and faster,
the colours wet and new.
The world so wide on the windscreen,
so narrow in the rear window.
That's where I used to live,
strange, to think of someone else
a slave to my old habits.
The straight lines peter out and,
at last,
it's only landscape:
moving, wavy, green
like you're painting it.
The universe comes from a long way in front
time-lapsing vast over me
decaying in my wake
finally small,
curled, dark,
gone.
On the CD player
Miles and Trane are still together,
on the brink of something new,
and the three of us in the car
are like a message in a bottle
cast in the sea.

Barbados
For Charles Christopher Parker, Jr.
29/8/20 – 12/3/55

Warm Barbados:
the slow surf piles on the beach like blue pullovers being folded away
and the lost umbrellas of palms
accept the breeze
and their own raggedness.
Oh, to sit in the sun
and feel my temperature move up
far from double pneumonia
and this rich white woman's apartment
in a Manhattan
still short of Spring.
Here there's only shivering,
being sick and watching TV:
the Dorsey brothers,
looking cold in shades of gray,
are all that's on.
Nica's friends knock at the door
and conversations go on in the parlour.
Some of her paintings occupy the room with me:
heavy framed, permanent impressions.
Here,
everything
is an investment.
Yes, I'll get this titled lady,
whose corridors look like the inside of a yacht
and whose whole life is Caribbean,
to send me into the Summer bound south
where men are dark
and art's all word of mouth.

La Madeleine at Vezelay

The medieval cathedral
at Vezelay
was a safe place to rest
on the way
to Saint John de Compostella
for the pilgrims and crusaders
pouring
like metal along a mold
southward to Spain.

Vezelay:
with its hill
and walls
and rain coloured church.

I'm not normally fond of cathedrals.
I tend to take buildings personally
and while they, mostly,
get the exterior right,
once the door is closed on the good taste of the weather
what is left is the viscera
divided into side-show chapels
featuring over-painted women
and their exposed organs,
the light flickering on them like
skirts that want to rise,
and tortured, emaciated men
playing on your sympathies.
They put me in mind of TV commercials
that spoil a fairly good film.

But at Vezelay,
where it's first gear going up
and first gear coming down,
inside there is only the stone
cool like a doorway out of the rain:
no bleeding hearts,
no pleading, impaled hands,
no colour:
a vision
shown with no advertisements at all
sort of religion
uninterrupted
or rather
not religion, but faith
in the specific gravity
of the rock.

I'd like to stop right here,
trading my admiration
for an epiphany
but I'm afraid
all I can come up with
is a preference
for good theatres
over bad plays.

Look,
I cannot beg the question:
why the building
when the acreage is divine?
Why trash the flat
and call it rent?
There's an answer

in there
as to why anyone would mess with
a perfect designer world
and it answers
everything else.

Is it like dogs building their own houses
in the backyards
of those they've befriended?
Or perhaps a sailor on watch
cupping his hands
around a lucifer
so that a mate can smoke in the wind.
Is it like Drake
leaving a carven comment
at Yerba Buena
to say that on a warm day
with the sea behind him
like a long green thought
he stopped to take on water
and claim a continent?

Is it the monks at Vezelay,
chrysalized in their habits
spiraling
upward
peeling the pomander of the hill
to build their base camp
of considered sacrilege

or me,
visigoth as the rest,
vandalising earth, sky, women, men
scribbling quick grafitti
with a drying pen.

The Moon

The moon
glows its sad "O" tonight
and you are its reflection
on my window.

I never see the moon,
its compassionate face
making the night a vast pieta,
but that I think of you.

Thermal Barrier

Utilizing the latest in thermometers,
litmus paper, heat sensors and barometers
I have come across one fact to which I may hold:
incontestably, I am warm and you are cold.
One really doesn't need engines so intrepid
to measure this affair as luke-warm to tepid.
So I shall remove myself from the equation
ordering brochures, planning a vacation
to spend country weekends with other romantics
who share my wish to forget entirely
the second law of thermodynamics.

Jack Savage

Jack Savage
was not his real name.
People like me
can't say his real name

and for many of the people who can
it means
victim.

So Jack translated himself
to us
as Savage.
It could have been something else
even
a number
(he wasn't the only one of his family on whose dressing room
hung a star)

but Jack chose a name
that would fit in,
a commonplace:
Savage.

His true name, though,
was drummer:
a keeper of time,
an arbiter of pace.

Sitting
in the middle of the band
among his kit,
his skill modulating the choice
between stick and brush

part
of a process
that was more than pulse or breath,
something better than victim or savage.

And many knew Jack
as a joker
for that was one of a number
of middle names.

The endless supply of jokes
given, initially,
as cartes des visites
exchanged prior
to dismissal
or trust.

But Jack knew life
didn't have a punch line,
that the jokes were symptoms,
not causes.

And now,
there'll be some fills
missing behind the soloist,
some fours untraded,
some cues unheeded,

some awkward pauses
that could benefit from a joke,
for Jack
is gone some place
where, hopefully,
humour
is not needed.

Vincent

I gave her my ear.
What more did she want?
The tail?
It could have been a more standard
payment
but the rent
took that
and the thatcher of chairs,
the baker of baguettes,
the postage for Theo,
the face and rough hands
of Madame la Proprietesse,
the chandler of canvas
and all the rest.

Is it day yet?
Are the pin-wheel stars quiet?
Can I leave for the fields,
packing into my easel
the only good things
that are here?
Oh,
and the pistol.

If it doesn't rain
and I've canvas enough
I can stay out all day
painting
above and below the line
in my horizon shaped pictures.
Among
the wheat and crows

who do not judge me,
accepting me
as another creature
who, on fair days,
comes out
and builds his geometric nest
to spend the light
staring.

If they did judge
what a looney
they would think me,
all that effort
and still one dimension short
"Poor Vincent:
we live,
he paints".

Meisonnier
paid a troop of cavalry
to trample a field for the affect.
I have
only my revolver.

The crows,
more courteous than the village,
speckle the field
like notes in a score,
they do not take offence
at the final report
just move upward
in a kind of te deum
to give me room.

Utrillo's People

Do not pity me my stick figure
and my lack of dimension.
Call me "smashed beetle"
if you will.
It is true I have never felt the wind
or heard the rain
clattering in the trees.
I am a facade
without organ or nerve
but chiaroscuro
do not pity me.
When you are rot
caged in a box
I shall be standing in this street,
beneath a spout of absinthe
that passes for a tree,
among buildings as fresh
as new made promises
telling some other
tubercular soul
why two dimensions
are all I want of reality.

Washing Up After the Last Supper*
*Title courtesy of Graham Rowlands

I never mind washing up alone:
the warm, soapy water;
the restaurant closed and quiet;
the platters and cups going in dirty,
coming out clean;

considering the night
and the customers:
one group,
a party of 13,
very strange.

Had to sit in a row,
all on one side,
we had to push together 5 tables to fit.
The waiters wanted to say no
(it's hard to serve that kind of arrangement and they were clearly not
big spenders)
but I told them to go ahead.
I knew who these people were,
religious crazies.
They could make trouble.

So there they were,
very symmetrical.
Why would a bunch of guys go out to eat
and then sit in a line?
Aren't they friends?
Don't they want to talk to each other?
How's the kids? How's the wife? How's the folks? Have you seen
so-and-so lately?
What about Pilate? Shouldn't he be more hands-on?
I mean the guy at one end
wouldn't know if the guy at the other ordered pork.

But, to be honest, there wasn't a lot of conversation.
The guy in the middle did most of the talking
and the others just listened.
Although how much the guys at the ends heard is debatable – it was a
busy night.

I was run off my feet
so I didn't hear much of what was said
but it looked like a goodbye party to me.
The guy in the middle got a bit pissed,
a bit maudlin,
(Can't think of his name to save me but I know the family. His father's
a cabinet maker in Nazareth and his mother's the ultimate Jewish
mom. The boy has been a major trial for them.)
I think he was going away
but where's he going to?
That little donkey's not gonna get him far.

They stayed late
but finally wandered off into the night
half lit.
And, of course, no tip.
A waiter comes up to me then and says
One of them wants the cup the guy in the middle used.
"Does he want to pay for it?"
"No"
"Sorry, we're closed."
And it's one of those drying on the drainboard.
What does he think? "give me the cup"?
That it's my last supper?
I've got bookings for 37 tonight and a bar-mitzvah on Tuesday.

"Give me the cup", give me a break!

You know, you can tell a lot about people from their seating
arrangements.

14 February
for Helen

The logo of love
dominates the newsagencies
and the sweet shops;

glossy red hearts,
like recycled stop signs,
name this noon of February
as the annual birthday of romance

and those who like their affection
folded in half
post their valentines
to addresses that, mostly,
don't accept junk mail.

You may, by now, have guessed
that this overrated, bypassable organ
won't be on offer from me.
No,
it's not my aging, rural heart,
like a half eaten lure,
that I'll trail before you

but the hand built terraces of a mind,
the artisan's quarter of the city,
the corner libraries and bookshops,
the sudden squares with statues
enamelled by bird lime and profound
from centuries of holding the same gesture,
the gardens like fairgrounds of mortality.

All the space within the dykes and walls
of this community
make up my valentine.
All its mysteries are human
and thus, amenable to,
but not assured of,
solution.

So here it is:
I offer you this set decoration of time
and a padded seat
on a rowing bench
in the galley of Illusion.

Il Postino

I am alone in Chicago.
Not my suit of clothes,
not my knowledge
(from batting averages to lyrics),
not the way to the airport
keeps me company
and like a traveller afraid of wolves
I stay within the fire-lit blocks,
the street map of this place
folded into a small square
by my age
and the anticipation of infirmity.

In lieu of reality
I go to a movie,
preferring a ceilinged night
to an unroofed one

and it works.
Coming back
to my pre-arranged room,
with its gift wrapped bed
and poisoned chocolate,
I consider the film,
Il Postino
about an old topic:
Neruda

and an Italian postman
who,
bending and straightening
his bicycle up the hill,
delivered the world to the exiled Neruda
until the poet, finally free as a letter,
was allowed home
leaving the postman to deliver Neruda to the world
as he had learned him from conversations over the mail.
The world listened for half a minute
and then killed him for it,
crushing him as they rushed for the exits.

So, in the black leather, Chicago night
tooled by sirens and car doors slamming
the film is like a cabaret on a dark street
a light over the door.
Is it dangerous to go inside?
Will language, compassion, confidence kill me too?
Are these things lethal?
With only a few
inoculated,
immune
or is it that the bigger thing, life

is simply worthless:
like a diary
where the printed dates
are the only entries;
like a sea
without formations of fish
abruptly changing their mind;
or a pants pocket
without coins
to mill?

In Chile
far from the foreign postman,
the chopper moves the camera back
leaving a tiny speck that is Neruda
to gather the vast disordered herd
of his Chilean days
and in the logistics
of stockmen and remounts

accept
the inevitable undomestication
of the rest.

Level Crossing

I'll bet she was late for something.
Snatched her bag,
left the house in a rush.
Just remembering to lock the door,
leaving the radio on.
Maybe she was going to meet someone
at the pub across the highway

or post an entry form
to a competition.

The northbound train,
however,
was on time
inevitable as the evening.

The Country Link Xplorer,
from Sydney,
doesn't normally stop at Baan Baa.
Just sounds its whistle
as it hurtles through the town
on its way to a larger dot
on the map.

She might have been distracted by something:
a dog in the road,
the sun in her mirror
at the wrong moment.

On the level crossing
at Baan Baa
she met the train.

I doubt she was ready for that
in the midst of her errand,
odds and ends still in the car
from the last trip.
The sudden cessation
with obligations written all over
the feed store calendar
hanging over a hungry cat
and the 9 people who were injured

traveling on the unfortunate lady's agent of death
didn't expect such a delay:
worried family,
annoyed hosts.

They've closed the highway at the scene
and I am in the long line
of vehicles
stopped at Baan Baa.
The lady's car
is still on the tracks
bent and crumpled
like something used too much.

The wait is long
but it's no good turning around
and going back.
In this country,
where ground is more valued than bitumen,
there aren't many options
on how to get from here to there.
It's a big dry place
with just a few roads,
a few links,
and one is obligated to cross
where death
comes to drink.

Typewriter
for Garry, for Judit

I dropped my typewriter
a few days ago.
It's old, as old as me
and it was a sharp knock,
but it's done all my best work
so I couldn't lose it.

It looked ok
and a few pecks
seemed to go alright
and though grieved
that it was a bit dented
and bore a new scratch
I was relieved that I still had it.

But now, some time has passed
and I find that there has been an injury
deep within the machine.
A few legs will not lift
to step against the paper,
an accent has been lost,
now and then
there are certain words
(though just at this moment
I can't bring any to mind)
that can no longer be said.

Salome
for Garry Shead

A command performance:
flitting through the pillars,
around the pot plants,
between the garish guards
to dance before the King.
pleasing him
and his bulging friends.

Herod's wife is my mother's sister.
I am part of her statecraft,
along with a general ill feeling toward all
and a view of loss as evil.
In a world where all things are not equal,
John, known as the Baptist,
should have offended someone else.

Instead, his moment in court consists
of me, appeasing Auntie and her grudge,
moving as an animal
amid this pack of torpid predators
to diminish her pique
and with my exposure
and the oiled rubbings of my thighs
kill a man
of whom, it is well known,
there are many.

I am a serif
minute in their calligraphy of intrigue.
I move to the music
that is the best that we have

and think of something else
anything
rather than contemplating those men,
who sweat in idleness,
and the eel pit of their thoughts.

I am sick of my youth and their age.

Oh, come and carve me into a wall
so that my petrified step shows nothing of wax,
nothing of wane.

The seventh evolution,
now I am naked
letting all see what was hidden,
nothing of artifice left but a few loops of valuable chain
and no one meets my eyes
their concentration being on haunch and teat.
I know why cattle are deprived of perception.

And here is the trophy,
the acceptance of which
maintains me nude in front of them
sweat runneling into my groin.
It seems I've won a severed head
of a prophet without …much.
Just another who won't meet my eyes.

Well I've seen him around
and this
is an improvement:
only the hair and beard are unwashed;
and for him, I suppose,
it's an achievement of sorts:

the ascetic extreme:
no nether parts at all.

But no hard feelings, Johnny
give us a kiss to end the performance.
Let this naked girl
put her tongue in your mouth
and taste your absence.

It's copperish,
the flavour of this gigantic mystery,
like licking an idol.
But as I bow to the notables adjusting their robes
I think I get it.
This head on a tray is your receipt, Johnny.
Death has paid out your faith.
Now you are truly holy:
Holier than me
and, finally,
holier than thou.

Christmas at 70

Some of the bulbs don't light anymore,
the glaze on the balls is cracked,
ornaments are missing, lost
from years of being packed and unpacked,

the tree's artificial and weighs a ton,
the music's worn down to the metal,
those who knew what the rituals meant,
departed, with more important matters to settle.

The great, blinking tower of tree
like a ship under night embarkation
is no longer a link to what was
but a firm demarcation.

But yet, I'll wear the holly badge
and rally those who still be
to chant the old slogans and sing the old songs
around the once again erected Christmas tree

continuing a combat whose cause
repetition makes clear:
we were born with an enemy
and the enemy is still here.

Lucifer

It began
as a small misunderstanding.
Nothing, really.

I asked him for clarification on a ruling,
as it affected this free-will idea I had
and he took it all the wrong way.

But, if we're being honest,
he always did.

I tried to reason with him and his cronies
pointing out that regulations made for empty planets
might not be applicable
for one
that is occupied.

But, no,
it must be one rule for all
and those who meddle
with things as they were
will just have to accept
the problems they have caused.

Lost
my temper there a bit
"God"
(and he took offence! Suddenly I can't call him by his name?)
"just because you and your mates
are happy tending
your rocks and checking out the latest crater
doesn't mean we all are.
Look,
whatever put us in this galaxy
surely didn't intend for us to just watch the asteroids fly by!
Why bother with us if that's the case?"

All their brows met in one straight line,
their mutterings would have been like thunder
if any of their planets had weather.

It's difference that's the problem.
Difference is too difficult
and it hints that somebody might have been fallible.
So, they make rules against difference (traffic signs for cats
and I am accused of breaking one.
(It's about here that they always bring up the Mars canal fiasco. They never mention that one of them misplaced Uranus entirely.)

So, you-know-who, put it to a vote
(What kind of GOD, I ask you, would put something to a VOTE?)
and you know their sort
are going to outnumber
my sort,
everytime.

I was found guilty of an unspecified crime,
lese majeste
I guess
and sentenced to expulsion from the presence:
exile to the planet
I had so hopelessly muddled

Now, I watch from the briars,
as, outlined against a blue grey sky,
Sneezy, Dopey, Grumpy, etc. and a very large Snow White
try to manage a world
with 20000 kinds of beetles, 3116 religions (not counting astrology),
481 games involving balls and 6747 cheeses.

They feel the need to take frequent vacations
to their dachas on Saturnian moons,
winding down by watching whatever is extinct
observing all the rules.

Often there's no one in charge

Often it's exactly as I planned it.

Lucifer: God's Response

He said that, did he?
Hanging around that shabby pool hall of a planet,
preaching revolution to the revolting.
Damn! He proves
that euthanasia is wasted on the old.

Just like him to claim responsibility
for freedom
when, if not for him,
it would have been so much more.

Not more freedom
but enlightenment,
creation without destruction,
choices,
not guesses.

But, because he couldn't wait
there was only a fraction of the evolution,
the procession left incomplete.

Impatient, like all first born,
and to spite me
he made a present
by breaking the future.

He deserves his banishment
lost among ruins
that, in the half light of that place,
he thinks are building sites.

The Unused Portion

Well, that's another idea
that didn't work out.
The Crowbar
that forced it into scansion
bent thought out of shape;
that image,
like a disguise
too big for the imposter,
didn't fit
and the ending …
I just never got to.

Isn't there someplace
I could send it back to
along with the unused portion
and get some kind of refund?
Perhaps the same concern
that's responsible for these urges
to make things up
will take it back
and make amends,
grant an extension
on my guilt
at not having got it right,
an extra
rectangular dawn
on my window shade.

Maybe,
the unused bit is the most valuable bit:
the unwound stanzas,
the ending unreached,

the meaning never made clear,
the part
the customer was going to help me with.
Worth their while,
maybe.

Here,
I'll just bundle up all the drafts,
false starts,
paper popcorn from the bin
and send it back:
not unlike
sending it out in the first place,
or applying for work
you don't want
(not the labour, just the wage),

or being an organ donor.

Or perhaps not,
there are difficulties
with giving up the unexposed film,
blank page,
clean litho stone.
After all,
the unused is always the larger share.
It could wither here
as well as there
and anyway,
when I've scraped away the fraud and hyperbole,
the unused portion
appears to be
me.

Ayrton Senna

All he could do
was drive too fast,

finishing where he started
over and over again.

Many of his colleagues couldn't even do that:
not able to maintain the precise repetitions
of the endless roundabout,
come to grief before a pie shop
in a working class neighbourhood.

The edited sorrow of the TV news
shows him sitting in his car before a race
covered, as in a Victorian bath tub,
just a head above the metal slipper;
or Tutankhamen in his case:
too gilded to be true,
the features squeezed
in the perspex door of the helmet.

The names you've heard
from some industry you're not knowledgeable of
are exotic:
a town and a number on a sign
pointing away to a foreign place,
(perhaps, I would recognize the car,
but never the face).

That they die, these names,
is always a shock;
that the machine is the danger

not the course;
that it is dangerous,
even for Gods,
to leave the circuit at speed.

Somehow, the anonymously delivered morning paper
makes me sad,
to read the bold black name of the well-known stranger
above the photo on the front page
of the largely intact car
and learn that it
and the wall
made something new of each other
killing only the man in his bath.

NEW & NEWISH POEMS 2015

The Unused Portion
(Alternate Take)

Now that I am an antique
I have considered
colouring my hair:
that white ensign of surrender.
But a lot could go wrong,
my friends (mostly dead)
could think me vain,
henna might not look well on me.
But the box the preparation comes in
consoles me with these words:
"If, for any reason, you are unsatisfied,
simply return the unused portion
and your money will be cheerfully refunded."

A win/win situation,
unfortunately limited to the cosmetic world.
Where
is the similar small print contract
dealing with the larger unsatisfaction?
The universal falling away,
the carriage ride that becomes
the dust it displaces,
the mountainous terrain of energy
ending at a flat-lined horizon?

There are the promises of the priests,
but like the promises of politicians
they seem too convenient
to be true.
And, besides, other times,
other places

had other promises
and they
do not appear to have been kept.

No,
regardless of all the varied guarantees and offers,
some have made their own arrangements.
The aging population of the caves at Lascaux
mixed their unused portions
into a pigment,
not too different in shade
from my hair dye,
and coloured their thoughts with it.
Leaving
on the walls of where they lived
a proof that they were bigger than their bodies:
the stone their art bruised
an implicit contract
insuring a balance
between the portions used
and unused.

After Neruda
(Puedo Escribir)

Face up,
the star-pipped cards of night
are endlessly dealt
and
this, finally
is the night
when I have earned the right to speak
the saddest words.

Perhaps to speak of the slightly stirred dark
the stars stitched to it like seed pearls
by what must have been
a country of maidservants.

Or the wind
performing its evolutions over me
like a morose
song and dance man.

This, finally
is the night
when I have earned the right to speak
the saddest words.
We took it in turns
the loving,
now I loved, then she.

On nights
somewhat like this one
I kept her between my arms
kissing bruises on her
the colour of the unfenced sky.

We took it in turns
the loving,
now she loved, then me.
Indeed,
who, seeing the steady look
of those great calm eyes
could have kept from loving?.

This, finally
is the night

when I have earned the right to speak
the saddest words
to acknowledge she is not here
to sense she will never be here.
That neither I
nor mundane shopping lists
or half-done tasks
will bring her back.
Like something more massive than
the moon
eclipsing the sun,
her absence has enlarged the night.
I murmur to my soul
to keep it awake.

No matter that she broke the parole of my love
this matters:
the night has stars,
I have no one.

This is all:
in the distance someone sings
in the distance.
Only my soul does not concede
her loss.

Any intimacy
is worth it.
To find her in my sight
and bring her closer
with the focus wheel
would do,
but my heart,
the beater,

cannot flush her into range.
I remember this night,
I remember it making spectres of those trees,
I remember you
and me:
we alone have changed.

I can say,
with some certainty,
that I love her no longer
and with the same certainty say
that I live no longer.
Maybe if I scream my goodbye
into the wind
it will,
somewhere,
blow past her ear.

Another.
They will take it in turns
the loving,
now she,
now he,
like figures in a medieval clock
that tells the time for me
as I cross the square.
I say again,
with some certainty,
that I love her no longer
and yet
I'm not sure I know
what's loving,
what's forgetting.

For
on nights
somewhat like this one
I kept her between my arms.
Only my soul does not
concede her loss.

Even though,
this is the final pain she will cause me
and these the final words
she will get from me.

The Peacocks
Composer: Jimmy Rowles

Across the grass
the improbably ornate bird comes
like the doorman
of a long closed hotel
wandering in Central Park.

Slow Marching,
dragging his train behind him
as if swelling a progress
or making a procession
always on his way
to a formal occasion

or not,
who knows why birds do things?

A ceremonial sentry
who never removes his uniform.

Wherever he steps
is a parade ground
with his formation of one.
The gravity of his pace
leaving time for us to impute
complexities
no doubt, unwarranted.

And just as you thought
this solitary trooping of the colour
was all there was
he stops,
looks at you
and opens his tail:
into a gigantic cockade,
far bigger than the soldier.

You open your mouth
to start a conversation
and he folds up and walks away,
leaving you shabby
and ignored.

By the way,
peacocks can fly,
but prefer not to
seeing it as undignified.

Killer Joe
Composer: Benny Golson

Comin' at you
out of the speaker,
a needle of red light
keeping track of his high notes,
here comes Killer Joe
ax
at an aggressive angle.

Behind him, in the neighbourhood he lives in,
someone's keeping time
on an abandoned car
while Joe tells you an edited tale of his life,
tailored sharp
like his coat.

As he walks through your room
other cats from his hood
shout out something
slightly insulting,
slightly nice,
and it feels like he's comin'
straight for you.

Here he comes,
Killer Joe,
struttin',
stalkin',
Killer Joe
come to take your life

for a minute or two.

Killer Joe!

Romance

We both know
that we are not the best we've known
or probably will know,
not the brightest,
not the best looking,
not the wittiest,
not the most well read.

But, I hope
that you are, finally,
the woman I can have this conversation with,
lay those cards
that we've both thumbed up for so long
on the table.

You know,
I know,
neither of us is a culmination of some process
of elimination,
not the best of the best
but the current cast
of a repertory group

So can't we relax,
get rid of a few lies
and enjoy the play

sharing the programme,
moved by bits of business
I've never noticed before,
guffawing at wit amplified by you laughing too,
surges of lust as the ingénue leans over

and the glimpses of your stockinged knees
silken in the dark,
new turnings of phrase that I whisper into your ear
of epiphanies so far unexperienced.

Going back
after the show
to disarray some room together,
half-filled glasses
holding our seats
so that in the morning,
still ajar from all the sex,
we can find our places
and resume the discussion
of when we liked each other the most

and who knows?
At some distant, wee-small hour of that conversation,
when age has ruined our makeup
and surprise has lost its charms,
maybe I'll die
in your arms.

A Letter from a Santa's Helper

I know we lived on the beach
and your clerical pay/ my unemployment
and cheap wine
has a greater after affect
than that out of our reach.

Listening to what you murmured
with my cock in your mouth,

it was vows and pledges and promises
good as a country song
though the words were slurred.

But, some nights I'd watch the small boats bob
with blotched paint and arthritic boards
and wonder where I'd left my tools,
my feet being pulled at by something as big as the sea
frightened me, so I took this job.

You said you'd follow, but now you won't,
can't live in the cold
with all the year-end rush,
all the conformity, the lack of skin,
sneaking hits on a smuggled joint.

Yes, it's like that, all pine, not one oak,
but, it's warm on the inside,
the fascists go to bed early
and, anyway, I was sure you'd know
if I can't fix it, it ain't broke.

A Malevolence of Mynahs

The morning light through the venetians
pinstripes my wall

and framed in the window
a single, yellow booted mynah
steps onto the green stage of the lawn
like Sportin' Life lookin' for Bess.

Masked,
wearing the uniform of the Brownshirts,
pacing with hands behind him
he stares into every shadow
seeking the meek:
up to no good.
Others,
in the same livery,
watch from trees and bushes:
a malevolence of mynahs.
Each a gesture, a call
within an ill-intentioned chorus:
eager to ring Alan Jones
with an ounce of vituperation,
deftly clawing the keys
to poisonous blogs,
anxious to lend a hand
at the rack.

If my cat
had any social conscience
he could put them from here
in an instant.

No,
he's too much like me:
fitted into the couch,
old movies on the cable
a black and white person
in a garish world.

A Clutter of Spiders

Clutter,
indeed.
A term appropriate
only in the nursery
I'm afraid.
You see,
we Arachnids are not very family oriented
given that, more often than not,
mom eats dad
and both consume the kids.

Well, it doesn't tend
to family outings
and albums strewn
with miniature wanted posters.

So now,
even if my siblings and I are in a room together,
we stay in our respective corners
affecting not to know each other.

But, in any case,
indoors is not for me.
I'm more a sporty, "Hello, Miss Muffet, how's your tuffet?"
kind of spider.

Find a well trafficked space
and spend time
perfecting my sticky dart board
and when someone tugs on the latchcord
I drop what I'm doing
to rush over and hug my guest

with crime scene tape
leaving them for afters.
I only have one other relationship,
birds.
They're my only predator
and I hate them 'til the strings bounce.
Oh, not because they hunt
but because they sing.

I make nets,
they sing.
If there was to be but one choice for me
why could it not be song?

Sometimes,
alone in my net
on a fine day
among the bird sounds

I yearn for bad weather
to break the cords
and leave me
with days and days
of make and mend

weaving away the sadness
that I have no right to
any more than song.

For John and Willie
Mr. And Mrs. John and Wilhelmina Bruchman

Once I had an uncle
and an aunt
who every Christmas
filled up the windowed end of their Hollywood house
with a green, great-coated tree.

Lights
looped its arms
like the winking braid
on a Latin American Dictator;
ornaments,
either elegant or complex,
end-stopped every branch
each
an heirloom within my uncle's family
or bought from shops
that sold heirlooms.

The packages
spilled at the base of the tree
were solid blocks of metallic paper
with monogrammed ribbons
wrapped by the clerks in those shops.

Once
I had an uncle
and an aunt
and **they** were the mystery,
the proof of the fantasy,
the true fictional characters
of my childhood,

living the life
that I could see in the background
of MGM musicals
and films with Billie Burke in them.
I didn't believe in Santa Claus
or God,

I believed in them.

Once I had an uncle
and an aunt
whose enchantment
time has ended on this summer day in Southern California.
No matter,
I will go home
and trim a tree,
carefully hanging
each decoration facing the room
and place at its foot
two perfect packages
obtained from a shop
that remembers all of its old customers
and I will sit before it
as if it were the last and best window
in a favourite advent calendar
reading the morse of the blinking lights
in that quiet room.

Memories of My Mother in the Kitchen

The breeze
blowing across the sink of soapy water
moves the kitchen window curtains about
as if someone were taking liberties with the skirts of the house.

The sink, the window
are two of the containers
of foreign material
that accompany my mother's alchemy.

Every component of the process
is known to me:
the strata of aromas from her limited menu;
the kitchen sounds:
the cutlery drawer moving backward and forward,
opening and closing the door
on a medieval battle;
the sharp alarm of china meeting
and leaving one another;
the grunts of the cutting board;
the applause of flowered hands;

the chair back between my legs,
the weight of my chin on my arms,
the balance my toes keep on the linoleum.

Take this from me,
the final keeper of this lore,
as a writing out of the incantation,
no part of which may be omitted:
A spell against broken things
and the loss of what you need,
and gates that fail to shut behind you
and road maps that mislead.

At Night

In the black
display cases
of space
light glints
on the dotted i's
and crossed t's
of the past

hinting,
in this vast exhibit hall,
of a darkened machine,
as bones
deduce a beast.

And in these relics
of previous worlds
now moved on,
twisted
in time's kaleidoscope
I see the fire
of someone else's day
(never the night)

and know
that I, relic,
am also a curiosity
to some other gallery visitor,
whose myths
run in the opposite direction,
who watches from the darkness
under a moon with a bad complexion
but clear conscience,

maybe
side on to Saturn,
the perpendicular rings
whirring
like a celestial buzzsaw,

who also knows me
only as fire,
who will never visit my local beach
on an overcast day
and see clouds curl-pile
in grey perukes
and squall
their sudden tears.

State of the Union
Or thoughts of an expatriate at 4a.m.
in the High Desert outside Los Angeles

Some mad rooster
is forlornly crowing through the night,
creaking like a loose gate
in a world
where there are no handymen,
insecure
in his ability to tell dark from light,
while from all the unlit yards
individual dogs bark
as if a vast audience
randomly coughing at an awkward moment in the play
and the passage
of truck trailers
is a surf

rhythmically visiting my ear.
A clock display on the bedside table
deals the low cards
in an endless game of solitaire
and I, at the end of a long televised day
think of a nation
conceived in Liberty,
dedicated to a proposition,
that is now
engaged in a massive close-out sale:
"everything must go;
marked down to sell;
make me an offer".

Everything must go,
except the lies.
So we'll keep the flag
and let the country go,
we'll board up the Libraries
and keep the bumper stickers,
we'll buy prejudice
and sell wisdom,
we'll lose the farm
but keep the name for the housing development,
we'll invest in last week
and asset strip tomorrow,
we'll pick up the option on the sitcom
and cancel life,
we'll market the system
and discontinue the solution,
we'll let you have generosity
and compassion as loss leaders
and we'll throw in absolutely free
for nothing.

But wait, there's more,
if you phone right now
there'll be a recording
to take your call.
Just leave a message
after the beep

and no one
will get back to you.

On my 60th Birthday
For Mal Morgan

Rain has finally come.
The lineup of blue surfer days
now has a damp, grey dero at the end
shabby against the bar of the horizon
cooling my garden,
allowing the shadows to come out
from under the leaves
to mix black
into all the colours
tempting me
to go out in this new climate
and walk among the plants.

Gardens are not art,
not poems, not paintings;
the placement of the wager
of the seed,
of the ground,
of the rain;

coaxing the pigment out;
sharing the changes;
rising in the morning
to find the disarrangements of the night;
the accidental shit on the carpet;
and in the bright season
a tree swirling a muleta of shadow
around it

is not art,
is not specimen slide,
is not freeze frame,
is not art.

For Eduardo Castellanos
1927-1999

We were born on opposite sides
of an uncommon border:
a cowboy
and a vaquero
and after two lifetimes
of droving herds of totally different days,
came to an exhausted halt
in Canberra,
a country town at a faded frontier,
with the town pharmacist as the sheriff.
There we often sat together
among the tree sentried streets,
the burial plots of lawns,
the traffic waiting in reception lines,
to swallow new wine,
and talk of our distant mates drinking in cantinas and bars
that stand on stained, disorderly streets;

with interiors
darkened by smoking and lies
and violence and regrets;

missing them.

What we had in common:
art,
populist politics,
disrespect,
grog,
meant that, inevitably, chairs would be turned over,
tables pushed back and chips toppled
but,
most rides home were quiet

as was the one today from the funeral
and though the sun was out, after many days of rain,
it was not as bright as I remembered
and this evening,
within the constellations that helped guide the great cattle drives,
there is less star and more night
and a safe journey unlikely.

Conceit Number 2

Transcendent,
she exceeds the holy hyperboles
were she there
she could have killed Lazarus,
plea-bargained Jesus,
and taken Saint Christopher,
the patron saint of travellers,
miles out of his way.

Pelleas and Melisande

Pelleas and Melisande sound great
but as for me,
I'll take Molly and One-Eyed Jake
when anything but the Holy Grail's at stake.

Travelling Together

The same equation
(infinite on one side, exact on the other)
that governs Baccarat, spin the bottle, and 2-up

Also determines the way sheep piebald the hillside;
and why splintered and splayed sheds, like tired hens, slump alone;
and clouds enter and exit from the sky like un-blue defects;

and who wins, who loses
in the wager of us.

Concrete Structures

Concrete structures,
vast, rounded, bare,
have the look of naked women:
the full fleshed,
pale, granular skin
of the wanton
divided by curving creases
ending in shadowed
doors.

Might not
Jupiter Erectus
walking among us once more
rape a power station,
bugger a dam,
orally assault an auditorium,
chat up a trade centre
thinking he had found
female
with the heft and pallor
of the Gods?

What
the result of his pain
and abrasions
on learning how unyielding and coarse
his new Europa was?
Thunderbolts,
drought,
darkness,
the horsemen summoned from their respective corners?

Or
no complaints,
no remonstrances,
no retaliations,
no refusal to pay the bill
just a tourist
who, silently,
won't come this way again.

Noise

Outside,
a crane kicks down
the wall of a house;
traffic
is lined up, like beasts,
to get in at some gate,
heat rising from them
in marcelled waves;
a plane
scrapes down its glidepath
to the runway.

But inside,
my bishop moves on felt feet
and sweeps the black queen
from the field of blood and shade.
The pawns throw up their hands
and flap the pennons with their shouts.

Berths
For Kate and Anthony

We start off in the water
then someone hauls us up onto a life raft
the currents and winds move us,
the vessels get bigger.
One day,
we look back at the ticker tape parade of gulls
fluttering around our straight wake
and we take on a crew.

With more on board
a larger ship is required
and the wake it deposits on the water
is not as decisive as before,
but the ports of call
become routine
and the voyage a milk run.

Unless,
the thin black arm and clinched fist
of a U-boat
displays its ugly heraldry above the field of a wave
and sinks us with calamity.

Or we break our bows
on an unyielding
bit of the sea
and tumble out of our depth
down through the fish
going about their shopping
to the place where vanished vessels go,
old razorblades lie,
missing socks end up
and bucks finally stop.

Mostly though,
the voyaging goes on
and the boats begin to diminish,
the crew disembark
until, one day,
we're in the water again
slapping around us for purchase,

weighed down
by the unfloating logs of our journey

we take them as we go
not rosters of where we went,
but a trip by trip
explanation
of what the wake meant.

Man, Dead Two and a Half Years, Found in His Flat

In his grave
there's no whispering or tiptoes,
the light's on and the radio's playing.
Outside in the Street,
cars drive to the intersection,
where there are no right turns,
and wait for the signal to change.
The milk bar cheats on its use-by dates
and the Herald takes back
the days that didn't sell.

The local population go on gift wrapping their lives
as offerings for others.
They don't miss the man
lying in his room listening to the radio.
When he wanted in, they let him in
when he wanted out, they let him go.

No one has taken him to some ghetto of the dead,
he continues to occupy
his small part of the community
mourned, to the limits of our civilisation,
by the filaments of the lamp
and the transistors of the radio.
He is immortal
as long as the rent is paid.

Jane Grey
For Robert Harris

As anonymous as a star
made barely distinct
by dark
are most

walking the mindless, double-back, evasive
patterns of their lives
in slower
larger ambits
than the ants.

Only some,
gone home
one night,
late,
happen to be opposite
the door
that suddenly fans light
out onto the street
and are caught:
Pupils large in their eyes
like archery butts,
surprise and fear
a scaffold
of the tendons in the neck,
the lines across the forehead
like a noteless music staff.

I think of Jane Grey:
An incident
between levee and soiree
a dropped, pearl seeded glove

becoming
an overturned sedan chair
like an embroidered box
for a discontinued item

and the disbelief at the jar,
at climbing out
upwards,
at the muddy valenciennes,
at the steady
pendulum steps of the silk
slipper,
at the cold
and the silence coming from
the block.

Never
to change clothes,
to be naked,
and love your lover
with your mouth,
to go from lust
to audience
and speak over the reek
of him
to the wives of peers.

Never to look up from a book
and see
at the turning of the year
a tree
like an illuminated letter
and lose the track
of the text
and forget all your fears.

Never.

Blues for an Empty Room

When you were lonely
I sat with you
when you were happy
I laughed with you
when you were horny
I laid with you
why am I left in this empty room?

When you were hungry
I cooked for you
when you were thirsty
I drank with you
and when you were tired
I just didn't bother you
why am I left in this empty room?

What more,
what more could I have done?
Every battle you wanted to win
you won
you had your cake
and you ate it too
what was there to do
I didn't do.

When you were wild
I coped with you
when you were a child
I comforted you
and when you were there
I needed you
why am I left in this empty room?

Lies about my Parents

My mother loved giraffes,
but she didn't work at it;
she loved
giraffes,
not directly
but more at an angle.

I always thought
it was because my father's favourite saying was
"halitosis is better than no breath at all"
and in conversation with giraffes
one tends to keep one's distance.

I think it was their imperfection she liked sort
of made, not born.
A creature
cannibalised from a childhood of cracked toys,
mended and remended
with unmatched bits.

So,
my mother loved giraffes
and collected them
to stand between the lamps and bookends
extended and alert
as if wondering where Africa had gone.
She had them in glass
and wood and plastic,
I liked the ones from India
with pieces of mirror

you could see
parts
of yourself in.

And now
on some veldt
like a gigantic nursery,
sky lifted up
out of the way,
she walks off along rows of
rocking-giraffes
like parked biplanes,
idly
pushing
them into agreeable nods

slowly squeezed into
absence
by parallel lines.

New Order

Sometimes I dream
I'm in Washington again, between
memorials
as it were,
the bottomland mist
gauzing the empty graves
of the heroes:
a city of crypts.

The bare winter cherry trees
lining the edges of the
Washington Monument
reflecting pool
are the burnt out bulbs
in an aging actress'
make-up mirror

and the capitol:
so much depends
on a wedding cake
left out in the rain;
the White House
with its coloured rooms too
dangerous
to have views.
In this dream
the fog,
the tourist sites,
the mezzotint weather,
are all.
No persons,
even I,
are present.

No passerbys,
no jaywalkers,
no demonstrators
on the boulevards and lawns
their raised placards
the mainsails
for an explorer's fleet.

En route
and detached
I see it

like the view from a missile
looking for a tyrant,
the grid of the streets
a map
about to be folded.

Sometimes,
I do not dream
nightmares.

Requiem

Moon,
I see you step on our pond
with your pale tread
and you find me alone.

No longer here,
that lady
with loose gown
and barrister hair

to brief
your trespass.

I Thought I Heard Buddy Bolden Say

Nobody knows
what Buddy Bolden said
because
he was drunk, they were drunk...
you know.
Bix died of it,

Fats died of it,
Eddie Condon
always played with Chivas Regal
sittin' in.

Bud Powell
played chords on the wall of his cell, and
Brew finished his trip
at the bottom
of some Danish stairs.
Trying
to prop the door open
with a bottle
you don't know
who might come in.

But,
there's things on both sides
and it's like Bunny said:
you can play drunk
'cause
you practice drunk.

Jazz

Jazz
is not
ice blocks
decaying together in a half-filled glass
while you're hanging out
in some
renamed club
where the owner can't
wait to switch on the juke box

between sets.

Nah!

Jazz
is the dark rectangles of speakers
in my room,
the measured spin
of the Clef LPs
like black holes,
the precise gesture
of discovery by the tone arm,
when it finds the right groove,
the message just
between me
and the guys.

Statuary

You
across the garden
only your Hellene
face
and scrolléd
alabaster hair
can I see.

For all
the rest
I must slide
my imagination
down
behind
the occult hedge

that stands
its fretted summer barrier
of enamelled leaf,
or winter palisade
of tangled branch
between us.

must cup
and form,
pulling
to perfect cones,
your breasts
like white fox faces;
must slope
and concave,
signaturing
by dent of navel,
your abdomen
like a marble basin;

must clasp
and stroke,
fluting
with sweet muscle
your doric
thighs.

Whilst I,
the stone of me,
must stand helmed
and greaved
with a thousand
years of armour

on my
pedestal
of time

by this eternally
clumsy fountain
and its knocked off
tumbled water.

Separate
from you,
in this garden,
only because
of distance
on gravelled paths

and the steel
marrowed
bone-white
of my period
and statue form.

Ros

No,
there's been some mistake
Ros doesn't do
dying.

Death
is for the more profound,
those who wrestle with it,
those who never solve it
but sense
the weight of it.

But not Ros
whose splendid ephemera
kept all of us young
and diverted
from the fact
that we are fashions
less and less worn,
ultimately hunched over our hangers
rows of us in dark closets
in houses
due for renovation.

In that movie
in my head
technicoloured Ros,
worrying about her frock, interrupts
story after story
before their sad endings

can be reached,

orders another bottle
or course
that
we can barely afford
and giggling,
never gets to
a last word.

Things for Which There Can Be No Blame

Children cry,
Wounded men bleed,
Old men die.

Dogs bark,
Cats are ungrateful,
Frayed connections spark.

The gin runs out,
Mattresses sag,
The wise doubt.

Plants like rain,
Judgements differ on your art,
Inevitably there is pain.

What's culled will be missed,
The last thoughts won't be finished,
The on-going account won't add up.

Not everyone will be amused,
The sea has no opinion,
Women and children will be confused.

Through ignorance will come shame,
Strangers will get lost,
We will apportion blame.

www.ingramcontent.com/pod-product-compliance
Lightning Source LLC
LaVergne TN
LVHW021559070426
835507LV00014B/1865